Celestial Whispers

Verses of Love, Longing and Luminescence

Ali Aryan

Made with ❤ on the BookLeaf Publishing Platform

www.bookleafpub.in

www.bookleafpub.com

Dedication

To all the wandering souls who have felt deeply, loved profoundly, and embraced vulnerability with courage. May you find echoes of your journey within these pages.

Preface

Poetry is more than mere words—it is the language of the soul, speaking truths we often fail to express aloud. This collection is an intimate voyage through love's passionate embrace, the quiet solitude of heartbreak, celestial dreams, whimsical fantasies, mystical reflections, and the raw beauty of nature. Each poem was born from moments of quiet contemplation, heartfelt longing, and sincere introspection. It's my hope that these verses resonate with your own experiences, gently reminding you that your feelings are valid, understood, and beautifully human.
May this collection not only speak to you but also inspire you to embrace the poetry within yourself.

Acknowledgements

I extend my deepest gratitude to those who inspired these poems—through love, loss, laughter, and lessons. To my family and friends, for your unwavering support and encouragement, especially during moments when words eluded me. To every reader, for welcoming my words into your hearts and giving life to my poetry through your own interpretations and emotions. Lastly, thank you to the countless poets and dreamers who have walked this path before me, illuminating the way and reminding me that we are never truly alone in our journey.

2. PART ONE : Passionate Odes

...

3. World's End, Our Beginning

The world may end tonight,
But with you beside me, all feels right.
All I ask is your hand in mine,
As my heart ruptures, captured by your eyes—
Mesmerizing, filling me with joy.
Dazzling me with your voice,
We could sit here for eternity.
Though the air is cold,
My heart is burning away,
Sinking into the ocean's depth,
Becoming its prey.
The stars have never shone this way,
As everything else fades away—
Burned by the light of the stars,
While the moon peeks through the clouds
To watch angels at play.
Everything longs for love
In its own way.

Deep, drowning, delighted—I felt it,
For the journey begins tonight.

4. Walk With Me

Walk with me,
Beneath the golden sun,
We don't need to be perfect—
For together, *we are one.*
Smile with me,
Let Cupid lose his aim,
For in your eyes, my love,
Perfection speaks your name.

Look at me,
As if I'm the first you've ever seen.
Hold my hand as we walk,
Blessed beneath this sunlit dream.
Walk with me,
Never let loneliness call your name.
I will never let you fall,
Don't worry, love,
I will never run.

Talk with me endlessly,
Till time itself is undone.
With every step, I thank the heavens,
For we walk beneath this sun.
Walk with me,
With love written in our fate.
I fear nothing in this world,
For you are near, my heart's escape.
And if they dare to steal your gaze,
Oh love, I won't let them take.

Fall in love with me,
Speak your heart so free.
With your eyes locked into mine,
Let's fall and never rise.
Walk with me,
Underneath the setting sun.
For now, our love's been written—
Forever, *we are one*.

3. Eternal Moment

In your eyes,
forever paused—
a heartbeat held,
a world uncaused.

5. Conveying Love

Should I convey my love,
Or should I let you realize it on your own?
With breath and death in balance,
Should I sleep alone?
Does love need proof to be true?
I'd rather stay with you and show it every day.
People speak, yet rarely mean,
For love, they have never truly been.

Lips cannot express love,
Nor can the voice,
But eyes reveal it when you see him.
It is the love you should seek,
True love hides within the heart.
One who loves cannot say it outright,
Fearing that friendship might fall apart.

Don't expect love to arrive at the right time,
It will come at the most unexpected hour.
Time may whisper that it's not right,
But love will always say,
"Everything's gonna be alright."

6. An Eternal Flame

Within the quiet depths of night, Our whispers breathe
and intertwine. A dance of souls in gentle flight, Where
your heart softly beats with mine.

Your eyes, a sea where stars reside, A universe within
their glow. In endless waves, our dreams collide, A love
the heavens envy so.

With every touch, an ember bright, Igniting fires within
my chest. Forever bound, in passion's light, Two hearts
in flame, forever blessed.

7. Morning Heartfelt

If you want to feel alive,
Fall in love with the one who sits beside,
The one who cannot bear to see you cry,
Whose heart extinguishes with every tear you sigh.
The one who will love you throughout your life,
Without conditions, *without goodbye.*

Fall in love with the one who screams when you cry,
Begging you to stop, with pain in his eye.
His heart sinking as your tears run dry,
Dedicated, devoted, delighted to see you smile.
He makes everything feel just fine,
As I stand forever by your side,
Loving you from the depths of my heart inside.

8. She is Walking Poetry

When I woke and saw you near me,

It was like the most beautiful thing ever to me,

Slowly did I fell in love with you,

Like a boat drowning in ocean of you

My eyes filled with tears since I loved you,

And I can't express what I feel,

But you could see it in my eyes whenever you are with

me.

9. By Mary, You Look Great

Love is when two hearts set the soul on fire,
When passion burns and sinks for a while.
When just a word can brighten your day,
And nothing else stands in your way.

10. Her Smile is Magic

I don't know about magic
But she could stop time
Every time she smile,
Making me believe
that *angels do exist* in this time.

11. Divine Gratitude

Should I thank you,
Or should I thank the God who made you?
On my knees every day,
I thank Him for blessing me with you.
Not just in gratitude, but in plea,
Praying He never takes you from me,
As I bow before divinity.

Light pierces through your cheeks when you smile,
The most beautiful sight my eyes could see.
Like the morning star that shines so bright,
Both in the day and through the night.
Should I thank God again tonight?

12. Love Without Conditions

Never love someone
On a condition,
Condition *changes* and so does love.

13. Divine Beauty

By Mary, you look great today.
Your cheeks are painted in a rosy hue,
And that smile—*taking my breath away*,
Your voice, as sweet as sugar too.
Innocence that carries me away,
If I write of you, I may grow old today.
By Mary, you look great today.

14. Midnight Wine Rendezvous

O Lord mine, beauty divine,
Filling thy heart with the love of her wine,
Stealing thy soul with the look of her eye.
Taking thy heart with the love in her eyes,
Taking everything that was ever mine,
Living in my mind all day till nine,
She became the paradise of mine.

O Lord, my
I expressed the love of mine,
With tears of love in thy eyes,
Made oaths to follow throughout life,
Making everything fine.
I couldn't express all love at the same time,
She became everything that was ever mine,
O Lord mine that beauty is mine.

15. The Day We Make

Stay with me—it's a long day.
The sun doesn't seem to shine today,
Still and staring as you smile,
Jealous, as it burns brighter today,
Trying to dampen our rage.
But who would tell him he can't burn us away?
It's you and me who make a beautiful day,
While others grow jealous and fade to grey.

16. When Two Hearts Ignite

Love is when two hearts set the soul on fire,
When passion burns and sinks for a while.
When just a word can brighten your day,
And nothing else stands in your way.

17. River of Moonlight

Smile little more girl,
You look perfect tonight,
Like a river *dying in moonlight.*

18. Drawn Hearts

Every day, she would draw a heart on my hand.
Sometimes, she wrote *"Mine,"* and I wrote *"Mrs. Mine"*
on her heart.

19. Words in Silence

I love those moments when she talks so much
That I take the honor of blocking her lips,
Just to feel the words in silence for a while.

20. Eyes That Ensnare

Her eyes were smiling,
I felt like a burning soul in her grace,
And I remained in her eyes until Judgment Day.

— *A person stuck between now and forever.*

21. Love Me to the Moon

Hold me without hesitation,
Love me to the moon and back.

— *If only I could say it to you.*

22. Pink Clouds and Smiles

My eyes are swayed towards you as you walk beneath
the darkling sky,
The clouds tends to turn pink by your smile,
My eyes gets deluded by the curve of your smile,
My heart becomes flattered and at the same time
dulcified.

23. Raindrop from Heaven

I didn't want to fall in love,
But you fell like a raindrop from heaven,
Falling on my dried soul,
And you smelled like the rain,
Kissing the flowers after a long time.

24. Wild in You

Wild side of me,
Loves the wild in you.

25. My Light, My Home

You are my light
and my lost way,
my drizzling night
and *my homestay.*

26. Better With You

You are my light
and my lost way,
my drizzling night
and *my homestay.*

27. Angel's Lift

Some days are worse and the rest of the days *I'm with you.*

28. Shadowed Devotion

Like a shadow,
I stayed with you,
fearing the day
you might step away
from the light
that kept us together.

29. All I Have is You

Is it good or bad
that all I have is you?

30. Just Love the Way You Are

Love you?
Love the way *you are*.

31. Rhythm of the Heart

You speak my heart aloud,
and it falls into my ears
like a rhythm—
one only *you can make*,
one only *I can feel*,
a rhythm only *we can create*.

32. She Outshines the Sun

Every morning as she slept.
The sun rose on her skin,
delicate—
like the moon rising,
without letting anyone know.
It tried to burn her skin
in its attempt
to warm her soul.
But she herself
was a spectacular source of light—
one the sky worshipped,
and the moon bowed to
every night.

33. A Longer Forever

And this time forever should *last a little longer.*

34. Heavenly Morning

She looked most beautiful
on a random sunny morning,
her voice—
an echo from heaven,
falling into my ears
like a *symphony*.
I became obsessed
with the thought
that even two eyes
can fall in love too.

35. God's Creation

The first time God fell in love,
He painted the whole universe.
The next time,
He created you for me.
And I became obsessed—
with the heavenly painted sky
that looked so real,
and with you,
who felt so *soul-warming to me.*

36. Bound by Fate

Tie me to yourself,
for this world once conspired
to tear us apart.

37. Forgotten Kind of Love

You and me and *a forgotten kind of love.*

38. Lily Among Thorns

Millions of people alive

But you my love Like a lily in a garden of treacherous

blooms

Your scent like the old summer day

No traffic or people – A dreamscape

In a garden, 'neath blossoms of lilies we'd whisper and

stay.

39. PART II: Lamenting Shadows

...

40. Wounded Knight

Sorry for being cold,
I am carved from wounds untold,
Scars that do not fade beneath the moon,
Oh Lord, these wounds!
They haunt me past noon,
As shadows gather before the sun is doomed.

Sorry for the fight,
I am a knight,
My armor torn in endless strife.
Many foes have left their mark,
Yet none could wound me like this night.
Oh Lord, these wounds!
I gaze upon the moon's embrace,
Hoping it will cleanse this pain.
Sorry for the goods,
I flee into the woods,
Lost beneath the silver glow,
Oh Lord, these wounds!
A warrior caged in fate's cruel hold,

Wounded deep where none may know.

"My Lord, do you suffer still?"
A voice so soft, a whisper still,
"You are wounded, and it's night,
Let me heal you with my might.
Do you need some wine?"
Wounds fade when touched by time,
Yet never have I seen such light at night,
Never have I felt so fine.

Oh Lord, this innocence!
The care that made me smile—
"Forgive me, my lady, for this plight...
Would you be mine?"

41. Silent Shore

Walking down the shore I see no one,
Waves roaring silently as lonely as sun,
Beauty stealing slowly my heart all at once,
Everyone is around but I see no one,
My eyes wandered with loneliness at the sky all, at once,
My heart broke silently and no voice did come,
Tears came out of my heart
And burned at once,
Rain fell down from the heaven but kissed no one,
Sun shining brightly but I see no light,
People went away one by one,
I walked with broken pieces that fell one by one,
Walking down the shore I see no one

42. A Glass of Pain

Give me a glass of pain,
And I will love you even more the same.
If there is some rain,
Let me taste a glance of disdain.
For my heart is lost—
Covered, conditioned, converged in someone's thought.
Give me a glass of pain,
So I may understand how it feels,
And I shall never do the same.
For the sake of unforgiven saints,
For the sake of Adam's mistake—
Give me a glass of pain,
And I shall remain yours forever.

43. Hurricane of Silence

When there is so much to say,
And no one to understand,
So many unoccupied thoughts,
So much occupied loss.
It's a drizzle when spoken,
A hurricane when felt.
And so, we choose to remain silent.

44. Faithless and Faded

Those who never loved,
Never cared,
Those who never cared,
Never believed,
Those who never believed
Became faithless and *faded*.

45. Unwanted Broken Flowers

Those who never loved,
Never cared,
Those who never cared,
Never believed,
Those who never believed
Became faithless and *faded*.

46. Defeated Warriors

We were defeated warriors trying to conquer the past.

47. Modern Love's Need

She kept breaking him,
and he let her—
for modern love
was measured in need,
not in *loyalty*.

48. Arranged Fragments

The truth is—
a broken heart can never be fixed.
Maybe you can arrange its pieces
in a way that it won't hurt,
and it will still work,
just fine,
with those arrangements.

Not whole,
but still beating.
Don't let it break again—
for each time,
the pieces grow smaller,
and it becomes harder
to piece them back together,
to make it work again.

49. Love's Casualties

Many starved from love,
Rest died from a heartbreak ,
Those who survived didn't had a heart left.

50. PART III: Celestial Reveries

...

51. Sprinkle of Stars

You and me—
a sprinkle of stars in the sky,
a grass field stretching to the moon.
A slow song,
dancing in the moonlight,
to the rhythm of each other's heartbeat—
in the forever.
Eyes reflecting the moon,
you and I,
sailing through the sky.

52. Moonlit Encounter

I saw you
with my lucid eyes
on a moonlit day,
and you were still
the most beautiful *soul*
I had ever met.

53. Where Stars Found Life

She was the kind
in whose arms the stars found life.
I was just stardust,
wandering in the dark.

54. Dark night

Where the nights were dark,
she *painted the stars.*

55. Chasing Stars

While we were *drowning*,
We still *chased* the stars.

56. Among the Stars

Among the stars we sailed
Down the heaven at par,
We both know that love lingered in our *eyes* and
heavens in our *hearts*

57. Sunkissed

The sun waits for the morning to rise,
Slowly and steadily, it kisses the night.
The sky blushes in pink for a while,
And stars celebrate by filling the heavens.
His light tries to dissolve slowly into her darkness,
Gently, steadily,
Making more stars appear in the night,
Holding her slowly and tight.

The North Star offers the darkness a path,
A way for her to reach and find happiness again.
But, oh! So many scars of the dark,
Oh! So many scars of the night,
That the light longs to dissolve into her night.
Yet, every day,
The sun waits for the morning to rise,
Slowly and steadily, it *kisses* the night.

58. Drinking Moonlight

She drank the moonlight.
The stars rose, jealous.
The sky went dark, and songs of heaven resonated in it.

59. Lunar Yearnings

The waves long to touch the moon,
Yet they know they never will.

Rising high, then falling low,
Drowning in their hope—still, they try.
Like a lone wolf howling at the sky,
Singing to a love out of reach,
Calling to the moon above,
Who will never be by his side.

60. Moonlit Approach

She came close to my eyes,
shining like light—
as if yesterday, *she was the moon.*

61. Falling Under a Dark Sky

Darker and darker,
the sky fell.
Slowly and silently,
we fell in love.

62. Stars and Scars

By stars and scars we found our way.

63. Seeing Stars

You are different—
Maybe because you see the stars,
While others only see the night.

— Or perhaps, I'm just overthinking today.

64. Night Sky Wonder

The beauty at the threshold of your eyes
Makes me wonder about the breath-taking night sky.

65. Dusk's Embrace

Nothing is more beautiful
Than a sky fading into dusk,
Embracing the *essence* of the night.

66. Sun's Devotion

The sun loved the moon so much that he hid behind
Just to see the moon shine.

67. Galaxies Apart

Call me whenever there is a *sink* in your heart,
Call me whenever the *galaxies* are apart,
Call me whenever you want a sigh of *bliss*, whenever
you get surrounded by *shadows* at par.

68. PART IV: Intimate Whispers

...

69. The Poet Remembers

I'm a poet; I don't remember the day I met you,
But I can describe how you smelled—*like flowers
blooming in sunlit depths.*
I can't recall what you said,
Yet I can describe how your voice felt—*like a
mockingbird with a sugared breath.*
I don't remember the day I proposed,
But I can convey how I felt:
Tears of joy enthralled me,
My feelings frothing like delicate foam.
I'm a poet, and you were the *thought* that lit my soul.

70. Mind's Creation

Maybe I've created you in my mind;
When I close my eyes, I drown in your thoughts.
When I open them, I'm astonished by your loss.
I try to sail into memories,
But my lids are forced open by your absence.
Maybe you aren't there—
Maybe you are—
Yet your eyes drown me in your thoughts.
Perhaps I've *created* you in my mind.

71. Where Eternity Meets Forgiveness

We will meet in *vain*,
Where eternity meets forgiveness and where there is a
little *rain*.

72. Sparkling Canvas

When her trust increased above the normal level,
Her eyes sparkled back at my canvas,
Her legs rolled over mine crossed with love,
Even lifeless flowers paused to gaze for a while.

73. Roses in Yellow Pages

Feelings mend into *roses*,
Which remained protected in the *yellow pages*
Of those books that nobody noticed.
They still smelled perfect, like the essence of love every
time,
As they were given in the days when love was expressed
through roses.

74. Unspoken Possibilities

No words were spoken.
No words were heard.
We were trapped in the possibility of everything,
and the probability of nothing—at once.

75. Lost Spirit Euphoria

I feel for you again,
like a lost spirit
wandering through the euphoria
of *hallucinated* dreams.

76. Deserving to Be Loved

The thought that she can have anybody,
and I can have anybody, scares me.
I know she deserves better,
but deserving someone better
is totally different from *deserving to be loved.*

77. A Heart Like Yours

Don't expect others to give in return as you do.
Not everyone has a heart like yours.
Not everyone understands what you feel.
Not everyone appreciates the small things you do.
But I do know how beautiful you are
And how lovely your soul is.

78. Infinity on an Unnamed Street

You and I, on an unnamed street—
unaware of the *universe*,
unaware of the *street* itself.
The sparkling light in your eyes
reflected in me,
as if we had forgotten to *breathe*.
Our hearts skipped a beat,
and somewhere between infinity
and your gaze,
I fell in *love*.

79. Attracted to Love, Loyal to Better

I'm attracted to love but *loyalty will be better.*

80. A Boy's Quest for True Love

A little boy searched for true love
all night long—
in people,
in stars,
in galaxies far, far away.
As he grew older, he realized
true love was never something to find—
it was something to *build*,
from *flaws*, *loyalty*, and *love*.
And so, he smiled all day,
gazing at the same stars,
now reflected in the eyes of the one he loved.

81. Chosen Over All

Be with someone who loves every bit of you, and chooses you over their best day.

82. You Are Poetry

Even you
are poetry—
to someone
who is hooked
on your *silent melody.*

83. Destination: You

I sailed through my thoughts
to escape you.
But the winds
whispered your name,
and the roars of my mind
called me back to you.

Then, I realized—
all along,
I had been sailing
through your thoughts,
and my destination
was always you.

84. Love for Myself

I don't keep all the love within me
because I know—
love is meant to be given.
But I keep a little for myself,
just enough
so *I won't be all alone.*

85. Shared Silence

I stay in my silence
until I find myself
falling for yours.
And together,
we end up in a world
where our silence
feels like *home*.

86. Love Without Judgment

I don't want to judge you—
you are beautiful in your own way.
Even on a tiring morning,
even on a bad day.

We need a love
that is independent,
unconditional,
and free of judgment.

Humans weren't made for love,
but the heart—
it was made by love,
and made to love.
So let's leave love to the hearts,
because humans will judge anyway.

87. Utopia of You

I replay memories of you
when bad thoughts try to break me.
You—*like a delicate dream,*
one I wish to wake up to,
with you still near me.
And so,
I drift back again
to the thought of you,
where in *the utopia of you,*
I remain.

88. PART V: Whimsical Serenades

....

89. A Glass of Red in a German Bar

As I went into the German bar
I ordered a red wine,
As good as it seem,
Should I drink you tonight ?
Like those drunk people
Overdosed at night,
You seem divine,
You look beautiful while being filled with love,
I should not drink you tonight,
I should adore you for a while.
As I went into the German bar
I ordered a red wine.

90. Half Devil, Half Rum

We are all half devil,
Half unopened rum,
With a *sprinkle of thoughts.*

91. Children at Heart

Let the child in me
love the child in you,
and maybe then,
we can forget
all the mature lies
we were told.
Maybe then,
we can fall in love.

92. PART VI: Mystic Meditations

Let the child in me
love the child in you,
and maybe then,
we can forget
all the mature lies
we were told.
Maybe then,
we can fall in love.

93. Walls Unbroken

It's beautiful.
The trees, the flowers,
the chirping of birds,
and the breeze *whispering to me.*
Although it's raining,
everything seems magnified.
But there is a wall blocking my way.
People said it's *all right*—
they were more worried about
why it's black and not grey.
I asked them, "Why is it blocking my way?"
I heard their *old lies.*

They seemed more concerned with colours and caps,
with how people should walk and speak.
I asked again, "Why is the wall blocking my way?"
They took holy books,
interpreted them in their own way,
and kept saying, *"Follow what I say."*
I pleaded with them to take the wall down.

They smiled and told me,
"We broke one long, long ago."
A little boy on the other side of the wall
said the old wall was *beautiful*—
it was built as a place
where people gathered in love and s*tayed together.*
I still hear his voice resonating in my mind.

Beyond the wall, I saw—
it was beautiful,
because they had no walls there.
Everything looked the same
from where I stood.
I heard their *old lies* again.
They spoke of love—
but they couldn't even break down
the wall between *you and me.*

94. Shifting Scenes

Hall is the same but pictures are changing,
People look alike but their intentions are changing,

Heart was never as it seemed,
People are remaining the same and not changing,

The small way they think,
Vigorously, valiantly, violating.

Those you thought would be with you are leaving,
Time is good but circumstances are changing,

Memories remaining the same but people are changing.
Like the sky simply fading,
People cry and do the same again,
As if they are born to do it again and again,

I am the same but people are changing,
Land remaining the same but houses are changing,
World remaining the same and times are changing,

This world is a stage,
Hall is the same but pictures are changing.

95. Path of the Unknown

Sometimes, I walk the path of the unknown,
Sometimes in her eyes, sometimes on my own.
While sailing in her gaze, I drown,
Surrendering to her dulcet poem.
It feels different when I'm alone.
The winds are soft, the moon is love,
Adrenaline chills my bones.
I'm lost in thought—
Better than drowning,
For my chin is up,
And I can hear my singing roar.
Maybe it's good,
Maybe drowning was even better.
But in the end, you know—
The loss is yours,
The loss is mine.
You would expect from others,
And I will keep walking,
Listening to my singing roar.

96. Solitude's Necessity

Sometimes, we need to spend time alone.
Not because we are self-centered,
but to find ourselves,
as we often get lost in worldly affairs.

97. Too Early to Pass

Some forever feel *too early to pass.*

98. Just Human

Even stars fall, I'm just a human.

99. Cloudbound Wonder

We sat above the clouds,
erring everything as a child's play—
wondering how vast life truly is,
and *how long we shall stay.*

100. Wandering Mind

Don't ask me where this road takes
For I have opened my eyes
Don't ask me what these words mean
For I don't know the difference between what's wrong
and what's right
I spend my day in yellow books and *dim lights*
ask me the way to reach a beautiful *mind, open-ocean or*
a silent morning site
For I had been above the stars and shone like light
I sail in my universe thinking who and why created you
and me?
I want to get lost a little more every day in my thoughts
and *silence starts to feel like me.*

101. Not Today, Death

I laid on the edge of death,
Death tried to console me with it's beautiful lies,
But I was strong enough to be me and stood alone in
front of his face which had made many
People deceased,
Not today I said,
Not today

My soul wasn't properly crushed,
My heart had to break a bit more,
My love wasn't properly given and my heart was
Just unsaid on many doors,
I had to go miles to be free,
But I was caged under the sky and dreams,
I wanted more before I reached the end to
Death's treat

I wanted to fight in the old age with wrinkles and a
burning soul trying to laugh and mourn on my stories,
I wanted death to see that my soul haven't been

Fully crushed yet,
It had been smiling indeed,
He might smile looking at me and I will still say not
today.

102. Reserving Love

In the end we all have some love left that we want to
keep for ourselves.

103. Alchemy of a Broken Heart

Take a heart,
break it,
then mend it again with love—
a pinch of darkness,
a small amount of light.
Replace his thoughts with a pen,
and everyone becomes a *poet.*

104. Timeless Keepsakes

Some moments are lost in time,
so we keep them in memories—
where they never change,
and we can visit them every day.

105. Unchangeable Truths

Smile—because there are stories of sorrow.
Laugh—because there will be moments when you'll cry.
Sleep—because some nights, you'll have to stay awake.
Love—because there will be times when you'll be broken.
Kiss—because there will be moments you'll regret.
Live—because one day, you'll be gone.
No one can change this—
neither you, nor I.

106. True Happiness

The goal is to be happy
Not to act happy.

107. Life's Paradox

Sometimes,
you can't be what you are in your mind.
You can't even express
what lingers on your lips.
Every simple thought
twists into a paradox.
And you, my friend,
curse life—
until one day,
you're too old to curse at all.
Then, death wraps its blanket around you,
and you realize—
it's too late
for a short trip back again.
And so,
you call it all life.

108. Hope in Hidden Stars

Even after all the tragedies,
the sun will rise,
and we will try again.
Maybe the hidden stars
can fill the space
between you and me.

109. Solitude of Overthinking

On many thoughts, I overthink.
In solitude, *I choose to remain.*

110. PART VII: Earthly Rhapsodies

...

111. Eternal Light in the Wild

I was there in the wild trying to find my soul,
My soul an eternal light,
Fell in love with the way the sun was dying as if he was
yearning to kiss my raptured soul.

112. Morning's Glow

As you wake up with a glass of sunshine,
Leaving behind the darkness of time past,
It's beautiful.

Your shine brightens my way,
Making my soul feel divine.
The way you kiss the leaves so passionately
Slows the clock,
Eyes closed—just for a while.
Although reality is more beautiful,
We close our eyes to feel it,
To keep it for some time.

Winds don't blow every day,
Nor do we see each other all day.
But it's beautiful in its own way.
The way she nurtures the plants
Instead of plucking them
Catches my attention every time.

And I lay every night,
Thinking about that warm summer day.

113. Winter Pink

She smiled, her nose tinged pink
on a cold winter morning,
entangling warmth
between her lips and mine.
And winter days
couldn't be more perfect.

114. Snowy Cascade

Snow wrapped around her
as if longing for warmth.
Her hair, like the *Cascades*,
rested on a *cashmere blanket*.
Symphonic winds,
mesmerized by her golden locks,
made me feel
as if it were Christmas Eve
every day.

115. Summer Breeze

I wish you could see her and feel the summer breeze
kissing you for the first time

116. Morning Conquest

I woke up early morning
My room dark, pinch of cold
My window warm-cold spring breeze
Chirping birds and fallen mature leaves
Distant silent voices encompassed me
A grin on my face as I rolled my demons upon my
sleeve,
I went once again to *conquer my unreal dreams.*

117. Fallen Leaf on Spring Morning

Winds held me, but I fell, Like a mature leaf on a spring
morning,
Falling onto an *immature sunny day.*